Beaded Macramé Jewelry

Beaded Macramé Jewelry

Stylish Designs, Exciting New Materials

Sherri Haab

Watson-Guptill Publications NEW YORK

First published in 2006 by Watson-Guptill Publications,
Crown Publishing Group, a division of Random House Inc.,
New York, NY
www.crownpublishing.com
www.watsonguptill.com

Library of Congress Cataloging-in-Publication Data
The CIP data for this title is on file with the Library of Congress.
Library of Congress Control Number: 2006923993
ISBN-13: 978-0-8230-2952-5
ISBN: 0-8230-2952-5

Senior Acquisitions Editor: Joy Aquilino
Editor: Marian Appellof
Designer: Alexandra Maldonado
Knot illustrations by Julie Mazur

Manufactured in Malaysia

First printing 2006

8 9 10 / 14

To my husband, Dan, thank
you for your support and
help with photography.

Acknowledgments

Thanks to my friends for their advice and help with projects.
Many thanks to the editorial and design staff at Watson-Guptill
for their hard work and dedication to this book.

Contents

Preface

Macramé is the craft of knotting cords—thread, rope, string, and the like—into patterns that are essentially geometric. Its first known use was recorded in the thirteenth century by Arabs, who called it *miqrama*, meaning, among other things, "ornamental fringe" or "embroidered veil." Eventually this art form spread throughout Europe and was a popular pastime among sailors, who crafted macramé objects while at sea and sold or traded them at their ports of call. Interest in the technique waned after the Victorian era, but was revived during the 1960s. With the introduction of a wide variety of new materials, today the craft is enjoying yet another return to favor.

You will be pleasantly surprised to learn that there are relatively few knots involved in macramé. Whether functional or decorative, today's macramé knots are essentially the same types used by those sailors in earlier times, who tied ropes and sophisticated net patterns with half hitch and square knots. Decorative Chinese knotting designs also employ some of the same basic knots used in macramé, although they are often called by different names; for example, what is known in the West as a square knot is called a flat knot in Chinese knotting patterns.

Once you learn a few simple knots, you will see that knots that look complex are simply variations on the basics. Intricate designs are created by combining basic knots to form patterns based on repetition, alternation, or juxtaposition, allowing for an infinite number of possibilities. In addition, you can create exciting jewelry designs by using a variety of cord materials, changing the number of cords, or by adding interesting beads and gemstones. It's amazing to think that the same knots used by sailors and Boy Scouts can be used to make gallery-worthy jewelry.

The projects in this book involve refined materials—cords made of leather or silk, beads that have been handcrafted, gemstones, stylish findings—to help you create jewelry that is not typical of the casual hemp- or jute-style macramé most people are familiar with. Some artists use macramé as part of an overall design to complement beads or other mixed-media components in a piece. Macramé, Chinese knotting, and tatting all use similar knots that are now being incorporated into jewelry design and other fiber arts. Rethink macramé; you may be surprised when you give it a second look and discover its wonderful potential.

Macramé Basics

Designing a Project

Designing a project is a matter of personal preference and depends on the style you want for the finished product. Choose a cord or stringing material based on texture, color, and weight (thickness). Test the beads you intend to use to make sure the cord will pass through the holes.

Think about whether you want the beads to match the cord, or whether you want the contrast of, say, strong complementary colors. It's important to make sure the findings work with the design as well; choose those that will balance the weight of the cord and beads to create a pleasing finished piece.

Cords and Stringing Materials

When you think of macramé, chances are you think of jute or hemp, which are almost synonymous with macramé design to the point that it is hard for people to separate the craft from these traditional materials. Hemp macramé chokers and bracelets abound at street fairs and malls. Macramé has a casual connotation due to the earthy, rough texture of both types of cord. However, since macramé is simply the art of tying knots, you can use any string or cord. Depending on the knot or the design, some fibers might be more suitable than others. The best way to discover which cord you prefer is to experiment and see how you like each type. Knitting shops and craft stores carry new and exciting varieties of novelty cords and fibers. This book explores nontraditional fibers and cords to give macramé a new twist.

Before you start your first project, you should become familiar with a few basic types of cords and their fiber content. This will help you to choose the kind that will ensure your work's success.

Nylon cord

This type of synthetic cord is very popular for macramé. Fine nylon cord, which is generically known as bonded #18-gauge nylon, is sold under the brand names Mastex, Conso, and C-Lon. It comes in a variety of colors from muted to bright. It holds knots well and is stiff enough to pass through small beads without requiring that you use a wire or needle. Another feature of this type of cord is that you can finish off the ends by melting them with a wax-heating tool or lighter, because nylon melts rather than burns. Nylon cord is also available in heavier weights, known as crochet thread or Chinese knotting cord, which can be used for larger items such as belts or purses. (The ends melt just as easily as the #18-gauge cord.)

Carded silk cord

Made by Griffin, a German company, this cord is commonly sold in beading shops. Though it's generally used for fine beadwork and pearl stringing, it is a wonderful cord to macramé with. A beading needle is attached to one end of the cord, providing an easy way to string small beads. The cord drapes nicely and looks expensive, especially when paired with semi-precious stones or pearls. The downside is that the cord is only 2 meters long, which can limit the complexity or length of a macramé design. You can, of course, incorporate additional cords as you work by hiding the ends under strategically placed knots. Other types of carded silk thread and cord are available in longer lengths than Griffin cord. These materials are appropriate for macramé as well, although they have a little less body and are softer in texture, looking more like thread than cord.

Other fine threads

These include cotton crochet thread, upholstery thread, and waxed linen. Each has pros and cons. Cotton, for example, is available in a variety of colors and weights but tends to wear over time. Waxed linen is difficult to use for some techniques, as the wax coating does not allow the cord to slide easily, but the upside is that many artists prefer it to jute or hemp. It comes in many colors and is available in different weights or thicknesses necessary for jewelry design.

Yarn and novelty cords

These materials can be knotted just as easily as when they are used for other needle arts such as weaving, tatting, knitting, and crochet. It's fun while exploring a knitting shop to think about how you would use a beautiful yarn in a macramé project.

A variety of stringing materials for macramé: wool and hemp yarn, ribbon yarn, nylon cord, carded silk, crochet thread, and leather cord.

Beads

Often the challenge of finding beads for a macramé design is coming across ones with holes that are large enough for the cord to pass through. Silk cord and #18-gauge nylon cord will fit through most small beads, while the hemp or jute cord used in traditional macramé calls for beads with larger holes, typically those made of wood or ceramic. However, plastic, glass, and metal beads with large holes can be used as well. You can enlarge the hole in a plastic bead with a hand drill or drill press if necessary, but you must take care to drill slowly so that the plastic doesn't melt on the drill bit. You can also make your own beads out of polymer clay or, as I did for the leather bracelet at bottom right on page 34, metal clay.

For an elegant design, think about using pearls or semiprecious stones instead of inexpensive beads. This will give your jewelry a sophisticated look, with the appeal of fine gallery-style work.

Look around at yard sales and thrift shops for costume jewelry you can take apart. This is often where you will find the most interesting beads that are perfect for macramé. Another option is to explore Internet auction sites, many of which feature a variety of vintage-style and hard-to-find beads, often designed specifically for use in macramé.

Here are a few bead terms you will encounter in this book:

- Seed beads are small, uniformly shaped round beads made from glass tubes. They are available in an array of colors and range from opaque to transparent and come in a variety of finishes. They're sized according to a unit of measure called "aught" (represented as a zero) instead of millimeters. A typical size might be 11/0. The higher the number on the left-hand side of the equation, the smaller the bead. For example, an 11/0 bead equals approximately twenty beads per inch, whereas a 6/0 bead measures approximately ten beads per inch. Common sizes include 11/0, 10/0, 8/0, and 6/0 (this last being the equivalent of an "E" bead).
- AB (named after the aurora borealis, or northern lights) is a type of surface finish on crystal beads that gives an iridescent rainbow effect.
- "E" is a common designation for 6/0-size seed beads, considered the largest type of seed bead.

Findings and Hardware

More casual macramé designs require only that you tie the ends of the cord instead of using a clasp. But if you use expensive beads and fine cord, it's nice to add jewelry findings to finish off the ends. Bead shops carry a variety of closures, jump rings, and wire headpins, to name just a few. An attractive button tied to one end of a design, with a macramé loop on the other, provides a simple, stylish closure.

Fabric stores carry hardware such as belt buckles, belt findings, and rings. You can also find purse handles and other hardware for purses, such as D rings and round or rectangular rings, which are readily available in fabric and craft stores. You might find interesting hardware items in the notions section, including upholstery supplies such as curtain and drapery rings, that might work for a macramé design.

Findings and hardware for macramé include purse handles, D rings, belt buckles, clasps for bracelets, headpins, and buttons.

Essential Supplies

The tools and supplies needed to begin a macramé project are relatively few. You may already own most of these items, as they are commonly used in the office or home for various tasks. Macramé is also a very portable craft, meaning that you can use a small clipboard, scissors, and a few clips to create a project while sitting in a waiting room or traveling on the road. The following describes the basic tools and supplies and how they are used.

Macramé Boards

To macramé, you need a board to support your work. Clipping your project to the top of the board holds the cords as you knot, allowing you to keep the tension even. There are a few options for boards to work on, as outlined here.

Foam core

This consists of a plastic-foam core with paper surfaces on either side and is found in art and office supply stores. You can cut it to any size and mount your work on it with pins. Foam core is available in various colors, which might provide a background contrast for the cords you're working with. Corrugated cardboard, although not as thick as foam core, can also be used.

Cork bulletin boards

Small, inexpensive cork bulletin boards work well for macramé because they are meant to have pins stuck in them. Also, they're available at a low price.

Ceiling tiles

These items, found in hardware stores, are very inexpensive and are great for macramé because they're sturdy and hold pins well. You can easily cut them to size with a utility knife.

Clipboards

Thanks to its built-in clip at the top, a simple office clipboard is handy for small projects, especially jewelry items.

Macramé boards from top to bottom: corrugated cardboard, clipboard, bulletin board, foam core, and ceiling tile.

Working Supplies

Other supplies needed for macramé are very few, which is one of the best aspects of this craft. Here is a list of common items to keep on hand.

T-pins

These sturdy pins will not bend when cord is pulled tightly around them. Use them to secure filler or holding cords by sticking them into your macramé board. Don't worry about when or when not to use them; it will become obvious as you work. I always keep a small box of these nearby when I need to secure a cord.

Binder clips

Available in different sizes, these ubiquitous items are found in office supply stores. The smaller ones should be sufficient for most jewelry designs. Use the clips to hold your work to the top of a board, or to clip a holding cord out to the side. Sometimes these are easier to use than pins, especially to secure fine cords.

Small, pointed scissors

This tool is the best implement for cutting fine cord. The point allows you to cut tight areas with precision.

Pliers

Sometimes you might need pliers to pull a cord through a tight hole of a bead if you have trouble grasping the cord with your fingers or pulling a wire through with the cord attached. Needle-nose or other small household pliers will work.

Tape

Masking tape and cellophane tape are handy when you have to juggle lots of cords. To hold cords out of the way, you can tape them temporarily to the board as you work through a design. Tape is also helpful for wrapping the ends of cords to keep them from fraying as you work.

Ruler

A ruler is needed to measure all of your cords and then cut them to the required length before beginning a project. A ruler can also help you determine in advance of starting a big project how much cord you will need. To make a sample to calculate cord lengths, measure an allotted amount of cord, then make a small sample pattern with it to see how much it calls for.

Wire or beading needle

A piece of wire or a beading needle will help you thread cord through beads. You can make your own beading needle by simply bending a small piece of wire in half, threading the cord at the bend, and using it to pull thread through a bead.

Finishing Ends

Because macramé is created with cords and fibers, it is important to finish off the ends to both prevent fraying and provide a neat finish. Here are three possible approaches.

Gluing

Hem sealants, such as Fray Check or Fray Block, which you can find in fabric stores, will give you a nice, clear coating that will seal the ends of fibrous cords. A clear-drying fabric glue, such as Sobo, is another good choice. For fine nylon cord, a jewelry adhesive with a fine-tip applicator

will do the trick; G-S Hypo Cement is one brand of this type of adhesive. It can be found alongside beading supplies at bead shops and craft stores.

Melting

This can serve as an alternative to glue for finishing the ends of cord made of nylon. Heating the ends of nylon cord melts the fibers, fusing them to prevent fraying. Wax-heating tools such as the Thread Zap and Wax Pen are battery-operated devices with a small heated element at the end; this allows you to melt fine nylon cord with much more precision and control than you would achieve with a cigarette lighter.

Hiding

Even after gluing or melting cord ends, it's sometimes helpful to hide finishing knots or the like under a bead when possible. This gives your work a professional look. One way to accomplish this is to leave cord ends long enough so that you can integrate them back into the design, securing them under a knot or bead before cutting the excess cord.

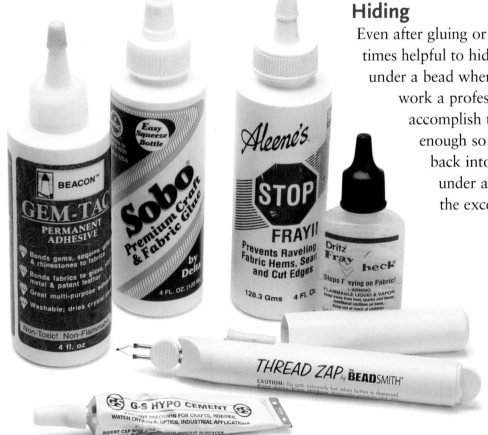

Knotting Techniques

Once you learn the basic knots, macramé is a matter of adjusting and keeping even tension in the cords you're working with to make your efforts look professional. The best way to accomplish this is to practice; you can do so easily and inexpensively using string or dental floss. One basic rule is to keep your holding or core cords taut while tying and wrapping working cords around them. Pin, tape, or clip holding cords as you work, and your knots will be even and consistent.

Macramé Terminology

The word *cord* refers to the string or fiber used to tie the knots for macramé. Various cords provide different functions for macramé design. Here is a description of each type and how it can be used to create a distinctive work of art.

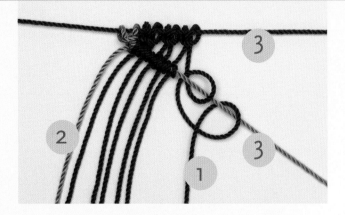

1. KNOTTING OR WORKING CORDS. These are wrapped, looped, and tied. The knots are tied with these.

2. CORE OR FILLER CORDS. Foundation cords, around which the working cords are tied. This type of cord often runs vertically throughout the design.

3. HOLDING CORDS. These are similar to core cords, as in having a knot-bearing function, but they often run back and forth horizontally or diagonally through a design. They also may be used as foundations to which core and working cords are tied; foundation cords are always horizontal. A ring or purse handle may also serve the same function as a foundation cord.

4. SENNIT CHAIN. This configuration of vertical knots repeats to form a pattern.

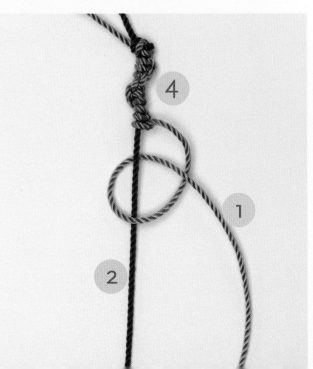

Overhand Knot

This is a very simple knot—the same kind used to tie your shoe. To tie the knot, make a loop with the cord, bring the end of the cord through the loop, and pull tight.

Barrel Knot

This knot is similar to the overhand knot. After making a loop, bring the end of the cord through the loop and wrap it around the cord at least three to five times, then pull tight. More wraps will give you a longer knot. The trick is to keep the tension nice and even so that one wrap isn't tighter than the others, causing the knot to bunch up.

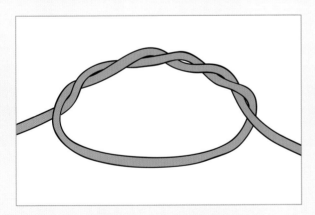

1. Make a loop, then bring the end of the cord through the loop and wrap it around the cord several times.

2. Pull the cord to tighten the knot.

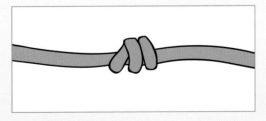

3. The finished barrel knot.

Slipknot

With a piece of cord, make a loop. Bring the working end of the cord up through the loop, making a second loop through the first one. Pull to tighten. This will cinch the first loop around the base of the second loop, forming a slipknot.

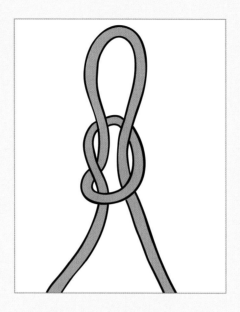

Lark's Head Knot

This knot is used to attach or mount a cord to a holding cord, ring, or other support.

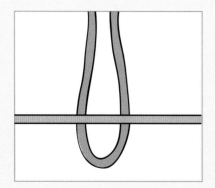

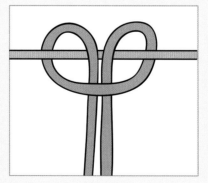

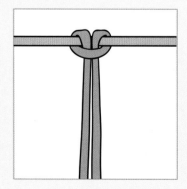

1. Fold a cord in half to create a loop, then bring the loop under the holding cord.

2. Bring the ends of the cord through the loop.

3. Pull the ends snugly over the holding cord to finish.

Lark's Head Sennit

This is a row of lark's head knots tied vertically over one or more core cords to form a chain, or sennit. Two separate loops are used. The first loop passes *over* the core cord, then under the core and through. The second loop passes *under* the core cord, then over the core and through. Following this procedure results in a nice woven pattern. If you see a break in the pattern, it's probably because you accidentally tied the same loop twice. In that case, pull out the knots to correct the mistake by following the over-under pattern along the chain. This knot is easiest to learn by practicing a few after looking at the illustrations.

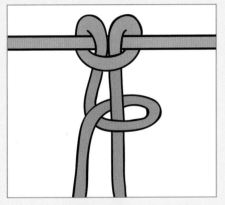

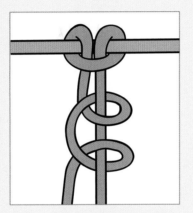

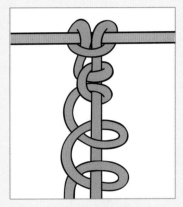

1. Tie a lark's head knot to a holding cord. Bring one of the cords extending from the knot (this becomes the working cord) up and *over* the core cord; next, loop it under the core and out through the loop as shown. This forms the first half of the knot. Pull this loop snug against the core cord.

2. To tie the second half of the knot, bring the working cord *under* the core cord this time, looping it over the core and through.

3. To create the chain, you always tie the first half of the knot over the core cord and the second half of the knot under the core.

Half-Knot

A half-knot is the first half of a square knot; however, it can be tied alone. If you tie a chain of half-knots, you'll get a spiral or twist. The example shown here begins with four cords mounted to a holding cord.

To tie a half-knot, bring the left cord over the two middle (core or filler) cords, like an L shape. Bring the right cord over the tail of the left cord, then under the two middle (core) cords and up through the left loop as shown. Pull the knot tightly against the middle (core) cords to secure.

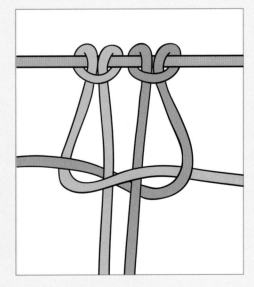

Square Knot (Flat Knot)

The square knot, also known as the "flat knot" in Chinese knotting, consists of two opposite half-knots. It is probably the most popular knot used in macramé. After tying the first half-knot (see the preceding illustration), tie a second half-knot directly under it. However, the difference is that this second knot is tied starting with the cord on the right side; it will look like a mirror image of the first half-knot. Start with the cord on the right, bringing it over the two center cords. Bring the left cord over the tail of the right, under the center cords, and back up through the loop on the right. It's helpful to practice this knot with two colors of cord to visualize the over-and-under path.

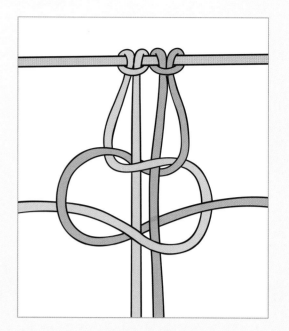

Alternating Square Knots

These form a woven pattern that can be tied close together to make a solid texture, or tied farther apart to make a netlike pattern. To form the pattern, tie a row of square knots using four cords for each knot. For the next row, pull the first two cords aside. Tie a square knot with the next four cords, which consist of two cords taken (or borrowed) from one square knot and two from the one next to it. The finished knot will sit directly in the middle of the two knots above it in the previous row. Continue down the row, tying knots that are created from the combination of the two knots above on the previous row. When you start the next row, go back to using the first four cords, repeating the row of knots tied in (or on) the first row. Continue to alternate rows to complete the pattern.

In this illustration, the first row of the pattern consists of 3 square knots; the second row consists of 2 square knots. The third row (not shown) would again consist of 3 square knots, and so on.

Vertical Half Hitch

This simple knot forms a spiral pattern when tied in a chain, or sennit. It consists of one loop. Bring the working cord over the core cord; loop it around and back under the core and through. Pull tightly. Tie each loop exactly the same way, being careful to consistently loop in the same direction, over and through.

Alternating Half Hitch

This is the same knot as the one used for the vertical half hitch, but instead of tying the same working cord over the same core cord throughout the pattern, you alternate the cords. Tie one cord (now the "work-ing" one) over a core cord, then switch so that the working cord now becomes the core. Tie the working cord (previously the core) over the new core. Continue switch-ing back and forth, tying one around the other to form the pattern. Keep the tension even as you apply it to the new core cord for each knot.

In a variation, instead of tying the cords around each other as you would for the alternating half hitch, you tie alternating working cords around a core (filler) cord. This creates a flat pattern rather than a spiral pattern (vertical half hitch) because you are using two cords.

Alternating half hitch.

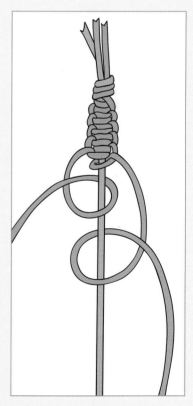

Alternating half hitch tied around filler cord.

Double Half Hitch

A double half hitch consists of two loops tied over a holding cord. The knots form a "wrapped" appearance over the cord. You can tie the knots horizontally or diagonally, depending on how the holding cord is positioned across the other cords in a row. To tie the knots, bring a cord (the first one in the row in this illustration) across the rest of the cords and pin or clip it to your macramé board to make a holding cord. Loop the second cord (in back of the holding cord) up, over, and around the holding cord, with the tail of the cord pulled to the inside (to the inside left in this illustration). Tie the second loop exactly the same as the first loop to complete the knot. Move to the next cord and repeat the knot, tying it over the same holding cord. Continue tying each cord along the row.

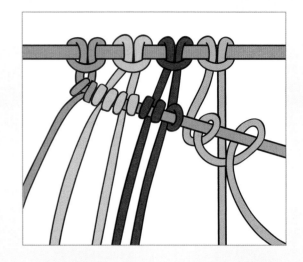

Three-Strand Braid

This is just like braiding hair; it calls for three strands of cord. Bring the left cord over the center strand; this cord now becomes the center. Bring the right cord over the center; now this cord becomes the center, and so forth. Follow the pattern, repeating left and right to form a braid.

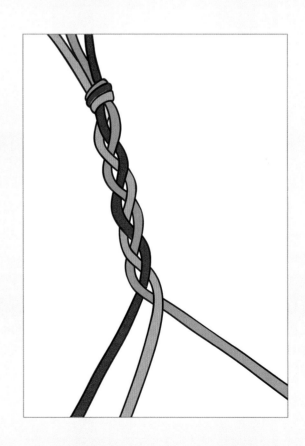

Josephine Knot

Make a loop with one cord on the left (here, blue) so that its tail end passes *under* the intersection point of the loop (A). Bring a second cord (here, gold) across the first (blue) loop formed and *under* its tail on the left-hand side (B). The cord then follows an over-under pattern as shown to complete the knot. Follow (C) and (D) in the diagram. Make the loops even on each side and adjust the size of the finished knot to your liking.

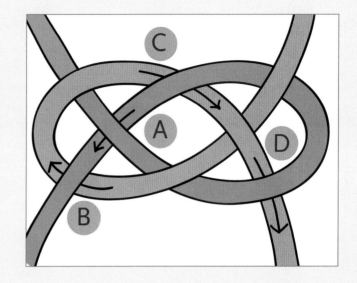

Wrapped Finishing Knot

This knot is used to neatly wrap a single cord or bundle of cords. It makes a decorative finish for the end of a cord, or it can be used as a slide closure for a necklace or bracelet.

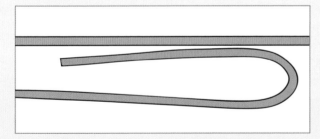

1. To form the knot, fold the wrapping (working) cord to make a loop as shown. Hold this folded cord (loop) next to the core cord that you will be wrapping.

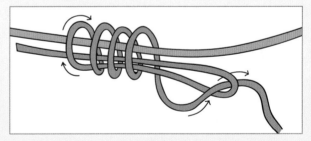

2. Start wrapping the working cord over itself and the core cord, wrapping toward the fold (loop).

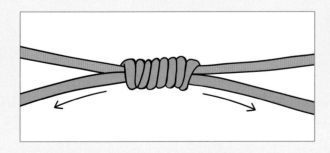

3. When you are satisfied with the number of wraps, bring the end of the working cord through the loop. Pull both ends of the cord tightly to finish. Clip off the ends of the cord and seal them to prevent fraying.

Macramé Projects

How the Projects Work

The projects in this book are arranged in a way that takes you from quick and easy to more complex. Although all are related in that they use the same basic macramé knots, some projects require a little more attention to detail than others.

The complexity of a project is determined by the combination of knots used or by increasing the number of cords. The more complex patterns involve steps such as numbering cords or paying attention to the placement of a knot. Others simply require more time to complete. No matter what, you'll be surprised at how sophisticated a single knot design can be, especially when repeated with beautiful beads and the right cord.

The instructions for most projects start out by knotting the work moving left to right. I did this for consistency and ease of following directions. Macramé books traditionally work in this fashion. But as soon as you get the hang of tying knot patterns, you may find that you prefer to work from right to left as you create rows of knots. In most cases this does not change the outcome, especially because most patterns are symmetrical— that is, one side of a design is often the mirror image of the other. Out of habit I actually prefer to work right to left, which does not seem to be related to being right- or left-handed (I'm right-handed). In some instances, I work from the center outward. This comes in handy when adjusting a knot placement for a centrally located bead or to create even spacing in a pattern.

Practice with yarn or some other type of cord to get a knotting rhythm going so you can determine what working method is most comfortable for you.

Note: Often I don't specify exact bead quantities for a given project; the number you use will depend on your own design preferences and/or the size the finished piece needs to be.

How Much Cord Do You Need?

A general rule of thumb for determining the length of cord you need is to plan for approximately four times the length of the finished project (eight times as long if doubled). Because some cords are tied more than others in a pattern, you will have to adjust the length to make sure some cords do not run out before the project is done. If the design is complex, you may want to factor in extra cord length.

Knotting Techniques Reference

 Overhand knot ▶ 21

 Barrel knot ▶ 21

 Slipknot ▶ 22

 Lark's head knot ▶ 22

 Lark's head sennit ▶ 23

 Half-knot ▶ 23

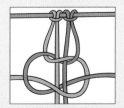 Square knot ▶ 24

 Alternating square knots ▶ 24

 Vertical half hitch ▶ 25

 Alternating half hitch ▶ 25

 Alternating half hitch with filler cord ▶ 25

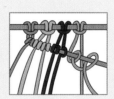 Double half hitch ▶ 26

 Three-strand braid ▶ 26

 Josephine knot ▶ 27

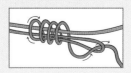 Wrapped finishing knot ▶ 27

materials

- ▶ Round leather cord (1.5–2 mm); cut one strand to a length of 72"
- ▶ Large bead with large hole for clasp

Simple Leather Bracelets

Round leather cord is available in an assortment of colors and widths and is a great material to use for macramé. Use simple knots and beads with large holes when working with round leather cord.

Lark's Head Bracelet

As a macramé material, leather cord allows you to complete a project in minutes. Handmade beads and neutral-color leather lend a warm, rustic feel to jewelry designs.

For the first step of this project, dampen the leather cord by soaking it briefly in water, then pat it dry with a towel. This will help soften the cord for tying.

1. Fold the cord at about one third of its length. The short end will act as the core (filler) cord and the long end will be used as the knotting or working cord. Tie an over-hand knot to create a loop large enough for the clasp bead to pass through.

2. Use the long cord to tie a sennit of lark's head knots along the filler cord. The lark's head knot requires a combination of two tied loops (or knots); for the first half of the knot or loop, the cord loops *over* the core, back under the core, and back through the loop. Pull tightly around the core.

Overhand knot   Lark's head sennit

KNOTS

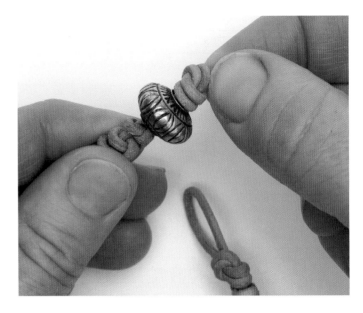

3. For the second half of the knot, the next loop passes *under* the core, back over the core, and through the loop. Tighten the cord around the core. Continue tying knots following steps 2 and 3 to complete the length of the bracelet.

4. Check the length by measuring to your wrist (an average finished bracelet is 7½" long). Finish by threading the clasp bead over both cords. Tie an overhand knot to secure. Clip the cords close to the knot.

The finished bracelet.

VARIATION

LARK'S HEAD BRACELET WITH MULTIPLE BEADS

You can easily embellish this simple type of bracelet with decorative beads. Slide beads with large holes over both cords along the length of the bracelet. Tie a few knots, slide a bead over both cords, and then continue tying knots, adding beads to form a pleasing pattern.

I made the silver beads for this bracelet using metal clay, forming them over drinking straws to ensure that the holes would be big enough for the cord to pass through.

materials

- **Round leather cord (1.5–2 mm); cut one strand to a length of 72"**

- **Large barrel-shaped bead or button with large hole for clasp**

- **4 round beads**

Josephine Knot Bracelet

The Josephine knot, also known as the "double coin knot," is very popular in Chinese knotting designs. It gets its name from the shape of two antique Chinese coins overlapping and symbolizes prosperity and longevity. Use sturdy cord or leather to hold the shape of this open-design knot.

1. Slide a large bead or button to be used for the clasp to the middle of the cord.

2. Using both cords, tie an overhand knot under the bead or button to secure.

Overhand knot   Josephine knot

KNOTS

3. With both strands, tie the first Josephine knot. To tie the knot, start with the cord on the left. Form a loop as shown.

4. Bring the right-hand cord across the left loop . . .

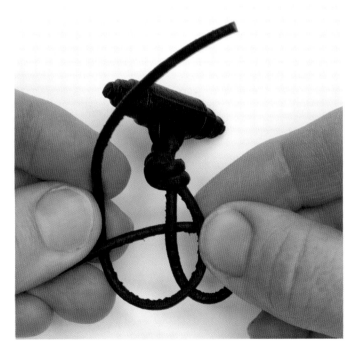

5. . . . and *under* the cord on the left-hand side.

6. The cord then follows an over-under pattern to complete the knot; here you can see the cord passing over and through the center of the cords.

7. Thread the cord over and under to complete the knot.

8. Adjust the knot to make the loops even on each side and correct the size of the finished knot.

9. Bring the two cords together and slide a round bead over both.

10. Form the next Josephine knot, and continue the pattern of alternating knots and beads until you have 5 knots total. Tie an overhand knot after the last Josephine knot. To make a clasp, tie another overhand knot some distance away with enough room to pass the bead or button through both cords to act as a closure for the bracelet. Cut the ends of the cord close to the knot. To clasp the bracelet, simply pass the bead or button between the cords.

Lampwork Bead Bracelets

This alternating half hitch bracelet features lampwork beads by Kirsten Peters McGrath. Lampwork beads are created by heating molten glass around a mandrel, a metal rod that forms the center hole of the bead. The width of the mandrel creates holes that are larger than those in other types of manufactured glass beads, making them ideal for macramé. Use colorful cord and accent beads to coordinate with the lampwork designs.

materials

- ▶ 5 yards chartreuse C-Lon cord (#18-gauge nylon)
- ▶ Shank button for closure
- ▶ 6/o seed beads for accents
- ▶ Assorted lampwork beads

 KNOTS

Slipknot	**Lark's head sennit**	**Square knot**	**Alternating half hitch around filler cord**	**Overhand knot**
		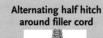		

1. Cut two lengths of cord, one of them 2 yards long and the other 3 yards long. Fold each cord in half to find the midpoint. About 6" above the midpoint of each, tie a slipknot with both cords to hold the work on a board. The 6" will give you space as you tie knots for the clasp, and will ensure that one length of cord doesn't become shorter than the other. Pin the slipknot to a board. Working with just 2 of the cords from one end, begin tying a vertical row of lark's head knots to form a sennit. Use the longer cord as the working cord, tying it around the shorter (core) cord. Remember, the lark's head knot requires two steps: The first loop passes *over* the core cord, back under the core, and through. The knot is completed with a second loop, this time *under* the core, looping back over and through. Pull the knots tightly, keeping the tension even as you work.

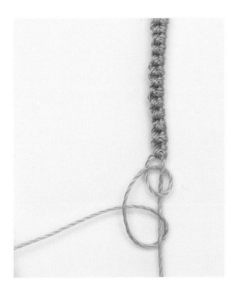

2. This photo illustrates both loops of the lark's head knot, with the first loop over and through and the next loop under and through to form the complete knot.

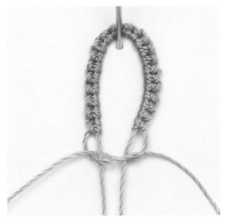

3. Work until the sennit is long enough to make a loop that will fit over a button to be used for the clasp. When it is long enough, pull the slipknot out and form a loop. Pin the center of the loop to the board.

4. Bring 2 middle cords to the center (these should be the shorter cords). Use the 2 outer cords to tie a square knot over the middle (core) cords. At left you can see the first half-knot for the square knot. After the second half-knot is tied to finish the knot, pull tightly to complete the loop (right).

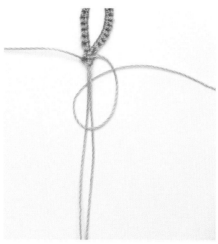

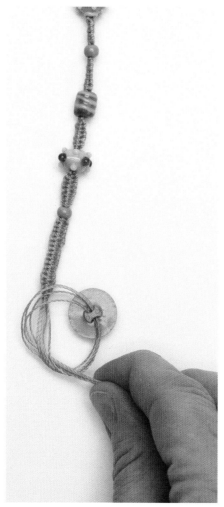

5. Tie a sennit of alternating half hitch knots around the 2 core or filler cords in the center. The knot is tied by bringing the left cord over and then looping under and through the filler cords.

6. For the next knot, work with the right cord on the opposite side and bring it over the filler cords, looping it under the filler cords and then through. The knots are exactly the same, except you alternate sides. The photo at right illustrates both knots to give you an idea of how they progress along the filler cord.

7. After you've tied about 5 to 6 knots, slide a large seed bead over all 4 cords. Continue tying a sennit of alternating knots. After 4 to 5 knots, add a lampwork bead, sliding the bead over all 4 cords.

8. Continue this pattern, adding beads to create a pleasing design. Measure the bracelet around your wrist as you go. When it is long enough to finish, slide the button over all 4 cords. Tie an overhand knot to attach the button. Then tie the cord around once more to form a secure knot as shown. Clip off the ends and use the wax-heating tool to finish them.

VERTICAL HALF HITCH SPIRAL BRACELET

This project, also with lampwork beads by Kirsten Peters McGrath, calls for the same basic materials as above; here the cord used is black.

1. Cut one piece of cord 1½ yards long and the other 3½ yards long. Fold the shorter cord in half to find the mid-point. Match one of the ends of the longer cord to the short cord so the lengths are the same on one end. With the two cords together, tie a sennit of lark's head knots to make the loop end of the bracelet. Follow steps 1 through 4 for the alternating half hitch bracelet (see page 39) to make the loop for the closure. Note that you will start tying the knots about 6" above or past the midpoint, working toward this point in the middle of the cord to keep the lengths as even as possible. The one cord that is longer than the rest becomes your working or tying cord.

2. To make the spiral pattern, the knot is one vertical half hitch. Use the long cord to make a loop over 3 core or filler cords. Loop the long strand back under the filler cords and through the loop. Keep repeating this knot to create a sennit. The knots will form a spiral pattern over the filler cords. Always remember to keep the loop the same direction, even when the spiral starts to form around the cord.

3. Every few knots, add a seed bead to the long working cord. Tie the knot around the filler cords after the bead has been positioned. To add lampwork beads with larger holes, slide the bead over all 4 cords. Continue the spiral pattern down the length of the bracelet.

4. When the bracelet is the right length for your wrist, follow step 8 of the preceding demonstration to attach a button for the closure.

Slipnot	Lark's head sennit	Square Knot	Vertical half hitch	Overhand knot

materials

- 3 cards size 4 light brown Griffin silk
- 3 cards size 4 carnelian Griffin silk
- 1 card size 4 garnet red Griffin silk
- Loop-and-toggle finding
- 2 large-holed cylindrical beads
- Small garnet beads
- Small silver beads
- Pearls
- Glue

Three-Strand Sampler Bracelet

This project consists of three separate knotted patterns that are combined to make a very attractive single jewelry piece. Silk is used, as it has the ability to "drape," giving this bracelet a soft, elegant look. To remove creases from the cords before knotting, simply unwind them from the cards and dampen them with water, then pat dry with a towel. (Just a reminder: Griffin carded silk comes in only one length, 2 meters; also, there is a beading needle attached to one end of the cord.)

For additional options, you can make this bracelet with a combination of any three strands of your favorite knot patterns, or you can add more strands if desired for a fuller design.

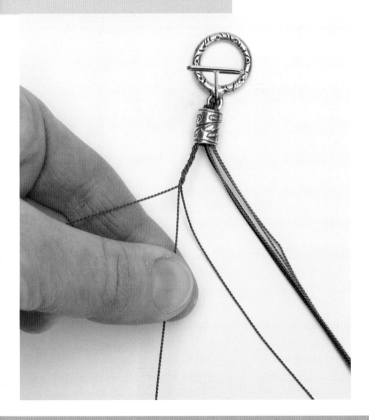

1. Prepare the cords as described above to remove creases. Attach the ends of the cords (not the needle ends; these will be used to string the beads) to the loop finding: With an overhand knot, tie 3 ends of the brown cord and 3 ends of the carnelian cord to the ring of the loop finding. In the center of these, add the garnet cord; fold it in half to find its midpoint and tie it onto the ring with a lark's head knot so its two ends are equal in length. The configuration of cords should now look like this: 3 brown, 2 red, 3 carnelian. Apply glue to all the knots to secure them. Slide a large-holed cylindrical bead over all of the cords, moving it up to hide the knots. Next, braid the brown cords for about ½".

Lark's head knot	Overhand knot	Three-strand braid	Alternating half hitch	Square knot

2. Add a garnet bead to the needle end of one of the brown cords and continue braiding. Create a pattern of braid and garnets, adding garnets along any of the three braiding cords as you work.

3. Measure the length of the braided cords around your wrist or that of the person you are making the bracelet for, being sure to account for the closure as you check the fit. At about 7", tie an overhand knot to finish the braid. Set this finished braided strand aside.

4. Now, with the red cord, tie alternating half hitch knots. This photo shows the right cord tied over the left.

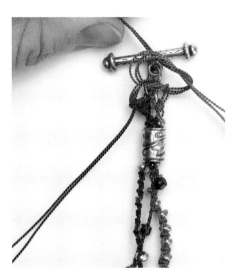

5. Add a silver bead to the needle end of the red cord. Tie a few more knots, then add another bead, continuing this way to form a pattern. Stop tying knots when the red strand is the same length as the braided brown strand. Finish with an overhand knot to secure.

6. The remaining 3 cords—the carnelian color—are tied with square knots. Pull one cord to the center to act as the core. The other 2 cords will be used to form the knots. Tie one square knot and then add a pearl to the core cord. Tie a square knot after the pearl. Continue a pattern that alternates one pearl, followed by one knot, until the length is the same as the previous two strands of the bracelet.

7. Finish by sliding a large-holed cylindrical bead over all of the cords; move it up as far as you can onto the finished strands to give you room to tie the ends of the cords to the toggle finding. Tie the ends of the strands to the toggle finding with square knots, securing them to each other with a few extra knots. Clip off the cord ends and glue the knots to secure. Slide the cylindrical bead that was moved out of the way up over the glued knots to hide them.

materials

- **Daria Multi yarn, color DAR-02; cut 2 strands, one 2 yards long and the other 2½ yards long**
- **Glass beads**
- **Headpins and jump rings**
- **Shank button for closure**
- **Hem sealant or fabric glue**

JAPANESE CORD BRACELET

This bracelet employs a beautiful variegated Japanese yarn that you might be able to find in yarn and knitting shops selling a wide variety of novelty fibers. A blend of cotton and rayon, this cord, manufactured by a company called Noro, gives your macramé jewelry a sophisticated look that sets it apart from pieces made with traditional hemp or jute.

One advantage of this project is that you can use beads of any size—including those with small holes—by adding headpins and jump rings to them.

Here's a brief account of how to proceed. To make the bead dangles, add a headpin to each bead, forming a loop with round-nose pliers to hang the beads. Make sure the loop is big enough to fit over the cord. Clip off the excess wire. Next, fold each piece of cord to find its midpoint. With the longer strand, tie a sennit of lark's head knots around the other cord (core cord), starting at the center. Shape the sennit into a loop to make sure it's long enough to fit around the button for the bracelet's closure.

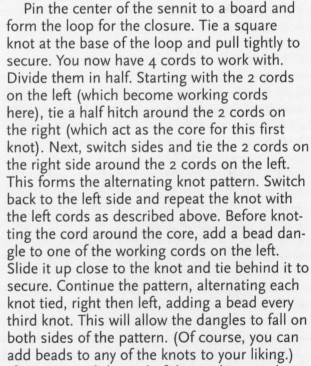

Pin the center of the sennit to a board and form the loop for the closure. Tie a square knot at the base of the loop and pull tightly to secure. You now have 4 cords to work with. Divide them in half. Starting with the 2 cords on the left (which become working cords here), tie a half hitch around the 2 cords on the right (which act as the core for this first knot). Next, switch sides and tie the 2 cords on the right side around the 2 cords on the left. This forms the alternating knot pattern. Switch back to the left side and repeat the knot with the left cords as described above. Before knotting the cord around the core, add a bead dangle to one of the working cords on the left. Slide it up close to the knot and tie behind it to secure. Continue the pattern, alternating each knot tied, right then left, adding a bead every third knot. This will allow the dangles to fall on both sides of the pattern. (Of course, you can add beads to any of the knots to your liking.)

Hint: Wrap a piece of tape around the end of the working cord to keep it from raveling as you work and aid in threading the beads.

Once the bracelet fits around your wrist or that of the person you're making it for, add the button. Split the cords into 2 on the right and 2 on the left. Slide the button over 2 cords on one side, then tie a square knot using both sets of cords. Pull tightly and clip off the ends, then secure them with hem sealant or glue to prevent raveling.

Lark's head sennit	Square knot	Alternating half hitch

Bohemian Earrings

Delicate earrings are works of art in miniature. Fiber and beads give the ones shown here a "Bohemian" style; these pieces can be worn dressed up, with a layered skirt and blouse, or dressed down, with old jeans, for a casual look.

materials

▶ 2 yards light green C-Lon cord (#18-gauge nylon), cut into 2 pieces, 36" each

▶ ½"-diameter jump rings (2)

▶ Ear wires (2)

▶ 6–8 mm faceted AB turquoise-colored crystal beads for center of each earring (2)

▶ 8/0 turquoise-colored drop beads (14 total; 7 for each earring)

▶ 6–8 mm faceted AB clear crystal beads for base of each earring (2)

KNOTS

Overhand knot	Lark's head knot/sennit	Square knot

1. Attach a large jump ring to an ear wire with pliers. Slide an 8/0 drop bead to the midpoint of the cord. Tie an overhand knot above the bead. Add an AB clear crystal bead over both ends of the cord, sliding it close to the knot. Attach the beads to the jump ring with a lark's head knot, using both ends of the cord. This knot will be tied at the bottom of the ring, opposite the ear wire as shown.

2. Bring the ends of the cord to the center of the ring and add a turquoise-colored crystal bead, sliding it over both cords to sit suspended in the middle of the ring.

3. Bring the cords to the opposite side of the beads attached at the base of the ring. The ear wire should be in the middle of the two cords. Start with one of the cords to knot.

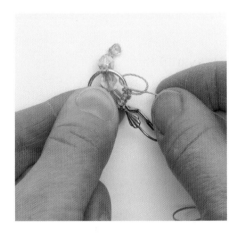

4. Tie a sennit of lark's head knots with each cord, working around the ring in opposite directions. This photo shows the knots working around the ring toward the beads at the base.

5. After tying 8 complete knots on each side, add a drop bead to one of the working cords. Slide the bead up close to the ring. After adding the bead, tie one lark's head knot to the ring to secure. Add the next bead and repeat the process of tying a knot after each bead until you have 3 beads. Repeat the process with the other cord to attach 3 beads to the other side.

6. At this point the entire ring should be covered with the knots and beads. (If you use a different-size jump ring, you will need to adjust the number of knots and beads to cover it.) Flip the earring over and tie a square knot on the back behind the beads. Pull tightly, clip the ends of the cord, and melt or glue them to secure the knot and prevent fraying.

materials

FOR THE ORANGE EARRINGS:

▶ 2 yards orange C-Lon cord, cut into 2 pieces, 36" each

▶ ½"-diameter jump rings (2)

▶ Ear wires (2)

▶ 8 mm faceted AB orange-colored crystal beads for center of each earring (2)

▶ 11/0 orange/pink seed beads

▶ 5 mm bicone-shape crystal beads (2)

FOR THE TURQUOISE EARRINGS:

▶ 4 yards turquoise C-Lon cord, cut into 6 pieces: 2 at 36" each and 4 at 18" each

▶ ½"-diameter jump rings (2)

▶ Ear wires (2)

▶ 4 mm faceted AB crystal beads (4)

▶ 8 mm faceted AB crystal beads (2)

▶ 8/0 turquoise-colored drop beads (12)

MORE EARRINGS

Orange variation: Attach a jump ring to the ear wire with pliers. Fold one piece of cord in half to find its midpoint, then tie it to the ring with a lark's head knot, beginning at the bottom of the ring, opposite the ear wire.

Bring the ends of the cord to the center of the ring and add an orange bead, sliding it over both cord ends to sit suspended in the middle of the ring. Next, bring the cords to the top of the ri ng to meet the ear wire, which should be in the middle of the 2 cords. Tie one lark's head knot to one side of the ear wire and then add a seed bead to the working cord. Tie a sennit of lark's head knots; add a bead after each knot, working around the ring toward its bottom.

Repeat the same with the other cord on the other side of the ear wire, tying knots and adding beads, until the ring is covered and both cords meet at the bottom.

This earring has a total of 9 knots and 8 seed beads on each side. Pull the remaining cords down and slide a bicone crystal bead over both cords, followed by a barrel knot. Clip the ends of the cord and melt or glue to secure and prevent fraying.

Turquoise variation: Attach a jump ring to the ear wire. With one 36" piece of cord, leaving a tail of about 9", tie a lark's head sennit, 8 knots in length, around one side of the jump ring. Slide the ear wire next to the knots and continue around the ring with another 8 knots. In the space at the base of the ring, mount the two 18" cords. At this point you should have a total of 6 cords dangling from the ring, grouped into 3 pairs. To the left- and right-hand pair, add a small (4 mm) crystal bead, tying an overhand knot under each. To the central pair of cords, add a larger (8 mm) crystal bead and tie an overhand knot under it. Then, to each of the 6 cords, add a turquoise-colored drop bead, tying an overhand knot after each. Melt or glue the cords to finish.

Lark's head knot/sennit

Barrel knot

Overhand knot

materials

- 3 yards C-Lon cord (#18-gauge nylon) per ring, any color

- Small cabochon, ¾–1" in size, per ring

- 4–6 accent beads—"E" beads or 6/o beads, about 3–4 mm in size—optional

- Small piece of light-weight leather or suede (can be imitation)

- Gem glue

- Sharp needle for sewing leather

- Clear nylon thread

Cabochon Rings

Rings are an unusual project for macramé, but with fine nylon cord they are very easy to make. The idea is to simply tie a chain of knots that fits around your finger. For variation, try using small beads around the ring instead of a cabochon, or attach a charm or button to dangle from the ring.

Square knot

Lark's head knot/sennit

Overhand knot

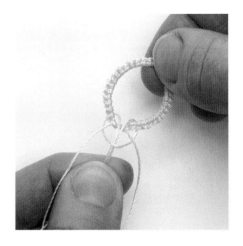

1. Cut 4 lengths of cord, one 36" piece and three 24" pieces. Begin at the center of the 36" cord and tie it around the circumference of the base of the cabochon with a square knot to secure. This will form a ring of cord on which to make the macramé "bezel."

2. Start with one of the ends and tie a sennit of lark's head knots, tying them around the ring until you reach the halfway point. Repeat with the other cord, tying a sennit of knots in the opposite direction around the ring. Continue until the cords meet, with an equal number of knots on each side, completely covering the ring.

3. At this point you will have 2 cords to work with and will need 2 more. Fold one 24" piece of cord in half and attach it in the center of the 2 cords on the ring with a lark's head knot. This will give you 4 strands of cord.

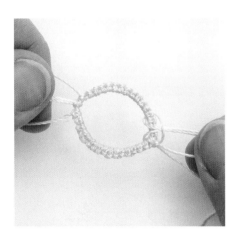

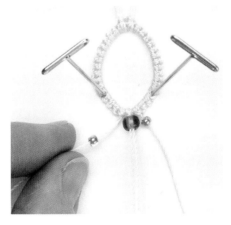

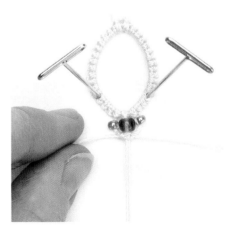

4. Fold the second 24" piece of cord in half and attach it in the same fashion to the opposite side of the ring, tying the ends over the square knot to hide it. This will give you 4 cords to work with on each side to form the band of the ring.

5. For the band: If you're using accent beads, add 3 of them to each side of the bezel, sliding 1 bead onto the central 2 cords and 1 bead on each of the 2 outside cords, moving them up close to the bezel.

6. Tie a square knot to secure the beads.

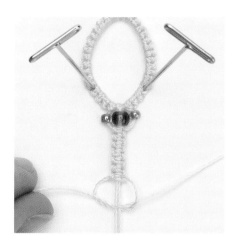

7. Make a sennit of square knots on each side to form the band, tying the outside cords over the 2 core cords. Stop after you've tied a few knots on either side; you will finish the length of the band after adding the cabochon.

8. Cut a small scrap of leather or suede to use as a backing for the cabochon, tacking it on with a drop of gem glue. After the glue has dried, cut the leather around the cabochon; leave an allowance of about ⅛" of excess around the edge.

9. Fit the macramé bezel over the cabochon, making sure it fits snugly at the base, with the strands for the band even on both sides. With a needle and clear nylon thread, whip-stitch the leather to the bezel all the way around. Tie a few overhand knots to secure the thread.

10. Tie each of the core cords with a square knot to fit around your finger, leaving the tying (working) cords out of the way. Clip about ⅛" from each knot and melt the ends of the core cords with a wax-heating tool.

11. Continue tying square knots with the free cords from both sides to cover the core cords and knots. Pull tightly and clip off the ends. Finish by melting the ends of each of the square knots to secure them.

materials

- 3 cards size 4 gray Griffin silk
- Silver loop-and-toggle finding for clasp
- 2 barrel-shaped silver beads with large holes
- About 15 freshwater pearls, 7–8 mm each
- 1 beading needle or piece of small-gauge wire that will fit through beads when doubled
- 1 strand 3 mm AB clear crystal beads
- Fabric sealant or glue

Pearl and Crystal Bracelet

This design combines freshwater pearls and cut crystal beads. The pearls are irregular in shape and size, while the crystal beads are uniform. The juxtaposition of asymmetrical and symmetrical elements here is visually and texturally interesting—a pleasing mix of unpredictable shapes and comfortable repetition.

When knotting this bracelet you may need to increase the number of crystals that surround each pearl, depending on how large the pearls are. Simply knot enough crystals to fit around each side of the pearl as you proceed.

1. Unwind the silk cord from the cards and dampen with water to release the creases; pat dry. Fold each of the 3 cords in half and thread them through the small loop at the base of the circular finding, pulling until the cords are even. You will have 6 strands of cord to work with. Tie an overhand knot with all 6 strands at the base of the finding.

2. Add a barrel-shaped silver bead over all 6 strands and slide it up to cover the knot.

Overhand knot   **Square knot**   **Lark's head sennit**

KNOTS

3. Pin the finding to your macramé board. Before you start to knot, separate the cords. Pull 2 of them down the middle. These will be the core, or filler, cords. Make sure these are the cords without the needles attached. Pull 2 cords out to each side (2 to the left and 2 to the right), leaving the core cords in the center. Make sure that a needle is attached to at least one of the cords on each side. (You will have an extra needle on one of the cords because you started with 3 to begin with; don't worry about using the extra one.) The cord on the left with the needle and the cord on the right with the needle will be the working (tying) cords; the other cord on each side will act as a core. To begin the first few knots, work with all 6 cords. Tie 2 complete square knots with both sets of cords on each side, tying around the 2 core cords. This photo shows the square knot consisting of 2 half-knots; you tie one half and then the other, pulling the cords to tighten around the core.

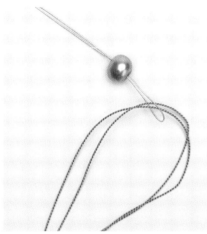

4. Add a pearl to the 2 center core cords. Since these are the cords without a needle, you can use a beading needle or make your own by bending a small piece of wire in half. Use the wire to thread the ends of the cord through the pearl.

5. Slide the pearl up to the base of the square knots as shown.

6. To add the crystal beads to the side of the pearl, pull one of the cords out to the left to become the filler cord (cord without the needle). Use the cord with the needle as the working cord. Add a crystal bead to the working cord and slide it up close to the square knots. Bring the working cord around the filler cord to tie the first loop for a lark's head knot. Pull until snug. Check to make sure the beads will fit around the sides of the pearl. If the pearls you're using are large, you may want to add an extra crystal bead to each side to make the design work.

7. The photo at left shows the second loop being tied to complete one lark's head knot. Don't forget that the first loop starts over and under, and the second loop is under, then over.

8. Add 2 more beads to the filler cord (for a total of 3 beads), tying a lark's head knot with the working cord behind each one to secure.

9. Repeat the same with the two cords on the right side of the pearl. This completes the pattern to be used for the rest of the bracelet.

10. Repeat the pattern by tying 2 square knots with all 6 cords, as in step 3. Make sure the knots are snug underneath the beads. Continue the pattern by adding crystals to the side cords and pearls to the center core cords as directed previously, followed by square knots under each completed set until the bracelet is close to the finished length.

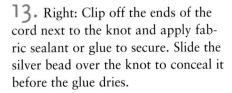

11. Measure the bracelet to fit your wrist and finish the pattern with 2 square knots (you may want to add a few extra square knots for a perfect fit). Slide a silver bead over all 6 cords, moving it over some of the square knots temporarily. Next, slide the bar toggle over all of the cords.

12. Attach all 6 cords to the bar toggle using a lark's head knot. Pull tight.

13. Right: Clip off the ends of the cord next to the knot and apply fabric sealant or glue to secure. Slide the silver bead over the knot to conceal it before the glue dries.

Chinese Knotting Cord Bracelet

This is a very quick project to make, since it calls for just a few knots and fairly heavy cord, in this case, Chinese knotting cord, which is made of nylon and available in a range of widths and colors. The basic pattern can be used to create a variety of bracelets in many different styles, depending on the materials used; for this reason, it's great for making gifts. It also has the added bonus of being adjustable in size, sure to please any recipient.

materials

▶ 4½ yards black Chinese knotting cord (medium size, 1.25–1.5 mm)

▶ 3 carved beads

▶ 2 pony beads

Overhand knot

Square knot

Alternating square knots

Wrapped finishing knot

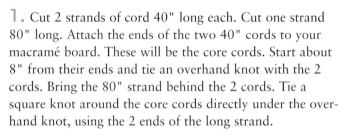

1. Cut 2 strands of cord 40" long each. Cut one strand 80" long. Attach the ends of the two 40" cords to your macramé board. These will be the core cords. Start about 8" from their ends and tie an overhand knot with the 2 cords. Bring the 80" strand behind the 2 cords. Tie a square knot around the core cords directly under the overhand knot, using the 2 ends of the long strand.

2. Now tie 3 alternating square knots; start on the left, using only 3 cords, with one in the center as the core cord.

3. Tie the next knot on the right side with 3 cords from the right, then go back to the left for the third and final alternating square knot.

4. Tie a square knot with all 4 cords (2 cords for the core). Slide a carved bead onto one of the center core cords.

5. Flip the bead and cord up out of the way and tie a sennit of square knots under the bead, enough knots to match its length. This bead required 4 complete square knots.

6. Bring the bead on the cord over the sennit of square knots to work the cord back into the pattern. Pull this cord next to the other middle core cord and tie a square knot over the core cords with the 2 outside cords.

7. Repeat steps 2, 3, and 4 to tie alternating square knots. End with a square knot using all 4 cords as directed in step 4. Then add the next carved bead.

8. After adding the second bead, repeat step 5. (This bead required 5 square knots behind it.) Bring the bead and cord back into the work. Tie a square knot, followed by 2 alternating square knots. Then tie a square knot with all 4 cords. Next, add the last carved bead followed by a sennit of 4 square knots behind it.

9. After adding the last carved bead, tie a square knot followed by 3 alternating square knots. End with a square knot.

10. Pull the ends tight, clip off and reserve the 2 outside knotting cords, and finish the cut ends by melting them with a wax-heating tool.

11. Tie an overhand knot with the 2 core cords remaining.

12. To make the closure, bring the opposite ends of the bracelet core cords together, placing them parallel to each other. Take a 12" piece of cord (reserved from step 10) and wrap the core cords with a finishing knot. Pull tightly, clip off the ends, and seal with the wax-heating tool.

13. Fit the bracelet over the widest part of your hand. This gives you a guide for how long to leave the tails for the closure. Add a pony bead to each end, finishing with an overhand knot. Clip and seal the ends with the wax-heating tool. To wear the bracelet, slide it over your wrist and pull the ends of the cord through the wrapped knot to fit.

SLIDING-CLOSURE BRACELET

Instead of using a wrapped finishing knot to make a sliding closure, Michelle Ross created one for this simple, elegant bracelet with a sennit of square knots.

After stringing beads onto a 12" strand of #18-gauge nylon cord, she laid the assembly on her work surface with the ends of the cords running parallel to each other, taping them down close to the beads. These cords served as the core for the sennit of square knots. She slipped another 12" cord under the core cords and tied a row of square knots to a length of about ½–¾", clipped off the ends about ¼" away from the knots, and sealed them. Next, she added a bead to each of the tails of the closure, securing them with overhand knots and finishing the ends. To wear the bracelet, you simply slide the cords to fit it over your hand, then pull the ends to tighten it around your wrist.

materials

- 9 yards brown Chinese knotting cord (fine, .75 mm)

- 1 carved cinnabar pendant bead

- 2 round carved cinnabar beads

- 10 glass pony beads

- 18" piece of orange red Chinese knotting cord (medium, 1.25–1.5 mm) for closure (optional; you can use the same brown cord listed above if desired)

- 3–4 small "E" beads and charm for tassel decoration

Chinese Cinnabar Pendant Necklace

Nylon Chinese knotting cord is fun to macramé with and gives you a very formal look. Bead shops carry carved beads to complement a design like this one; such beads are commonly available in cinnabar, a rust red color, but also come in black, tan, and jade. Make sure the holes in the beads will be large enough for the width of the cord you are using for the project.

1. Far left: Cut 1 yard of brown cord for the pendant piece, and cut 4 cords, 2 yards long each, for the necklace. Begin by attaching the pendant to the center of the 4 necklace cords. Cut the single yard of cord in half and thread the ends of the 2 cords up through the bottom of the pendant bead, looping over the midpoint of the 4 cords and back through the pendant. Pull the cords (4 ends) even at the base of the pendant, and secure with an overhand knot. Trim the ends to a length of about 6" to finish later.

2. Left: Begin on one side of the pendant by tying a sennit of alternating half hitch knots with all 4 cords. Divide the cords into 2 groups of 2. Tie 2 of the cords as though they were one over the other 2, then switch and repeat with the other 2 to form the knotted pattern. Tie about a 1" length of knots.

Overhand knot   **Alternating half hitch**   **Vertical half hitch**   **Wrapped finishing knot**

3. Repeat the knotted pattern in step 2 for the other side of the pendant. Then add 1 pony bead, 1 round cinnabar bead, and 1 pony bead to each side.

4. On one side of the necklace, split the strands of cord into 2 sections of 2 cords each. With one section, tie a sennit of vertical half hitch knots, using one cord as the working cord, tying it around the other cord. This will form a spiral pattern. Tie the pattern for about 1¼". Repeat with the other section of 2 cords. This will give you 2 spiral-patterned strands on one side of the necklace.

6. After completing the second section of spiraled cords, add another pony bead. Finish the length of the necklace by tying alternating half hitch knots—as in step 2—for another 3", ending with an overhand knot with all 4 cords. Repeat steps 4 through 6 to finish the other side of the necklace.

5. Tie an overhand knot with all 4 cords. Add a pony bead, followed by another overhand knot. Next, before you continue to create another section of half hitch knots to form a spiral pattern, switch the cords used for the previous set so that the shorter ones serve as core cords and the longer ones serve as knotting cords. This is to ensure that you won't run out of cord. Then repeat steps 4 and 5.

7. To make the adjustable closure: Bring the ends of the necklace cords from opposite sides, laying them parallel to each other. Fold the 18" piece of orange red cord a few inches from its end to make a loop, and lay this above the necklace cords.

8. Begin wrapping the tail of the orange cord around the brown cords, working toward the loop.

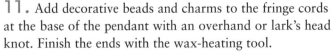

9. Pull the end of the tail through the loop and pull tightly to cinch the knot around the brown cords.

10. After completing the wrapped finishing knot, clip off its ends and melt them with a wax-heating tool to secure. Pull the necklace cords through the wrapped knot and make sure the ends of the necklace are long enough to fit over your head. Finish the ends of the necklace cords by adding a pony bead to each, tying an overhand knot to secure. Melt the ends of the cord to prevent fraying.

11. Add decorative beads and charms to the fringe cords at the base of the pendant with an overhand or lark's head knot. Finish the ends with the wax-heating tool.

materials

- 12 yards light blue C-Lon cord (#18-gauge nylon)
- Button for loop closure
- Freshwater pearls (number for project depends on size)
- Labradorite stone beads in faceted button shapes (number for project depends on size)
- Small crochet hook

Mermaid Necklace

The visual inspiration for this necklace was foaming waves rolling up on the seashore, which I captured by using a combination of pearls and natural, irregularly shaped light blue stones to give the design an organic feel. A netted pattern of knots completes the marine look. If you can find seashells with holes in them, you may want to add a few to the design as an extra embellishment.

1. Cut a piece of cord 2 yards long to use as the core cord to begin the loop closure of the necklace. Leave this as a single cord; do not double it. The working cord will be a single cord as well. For now, leave the working cord on the spool until you have started forming the necklace. Unspool a little more than 1 yard from the roll to use as the working cord. Hold the end of the core cord even with the end of the working cord from the spool. Measure 1 yard from the ends to mark the place to begin knotting to form the loop for the closure. Hint: Use an elastic band around the roll to keep the working cord from unspooling as you work. Begin tying a sennit of lark's head knots with the working cord (spool), tying it around the core. Tie enough knots to create a chain that's long enough to make a loop that will fit over the button to be used for the closure. The photo at far left shows the roll of cord being passed under the core to form the knots.

2. Form the loop for the closure with the sennit of knots to fit over the button. Now you have 4 cords at the bottom of the loop. At the base of the loop, tie a square knot over the 2 center (core) cords.

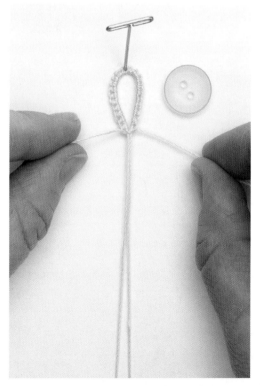

Lark's head knot/sennit	Square knot	Alternating square knots	Overhand knot	Barrel knot

KNOTS

3. Use the cord from the roll as the working cord to form the knots for the necklace. Continue tying a sennit of lark's head knots over the remaining 3 cords, which now serve as the core. Tie enough knots to form a length of about 1½".

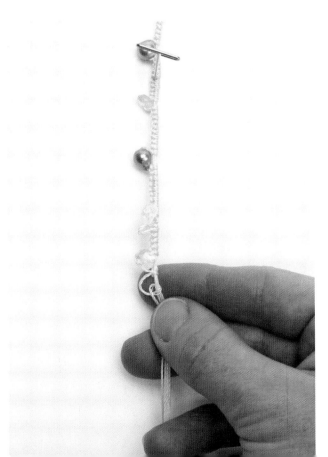

4. Measure and unroll about 5 yards from the working spool and cut. This will allow you to add beads to the cord as you work. Add beads to the cut end, starting with a pearl followed by a single labradorite bead. Thread on 7 beads, alternating them (pearl and labradorite) to the end of the working cord. To add beads as you knot, slide one up from the working cord close to the last knot tied. Tie 10 lark's head knots between each bead.

5. For the middle of the necklace, continue using the single working cord, unspooling cord as needed to add beads. You will use all labradorite beads instead of alternating with pearls for this section. Instead of simply tying lark's head knots as in step 4, here you will form picots—small loops of cord to which you will later connect other cords. First, add a labradorite bead and tie one lark's head knot to secure it. Then, to form the picot, leave the working cord loose to make a loop as you begin to tie the next lark's head knot. This photo shows a picot loop being tied with the first half of the lark's head knot. (This is the second picot on the necklace; you can see the first one completed previously in the row.)

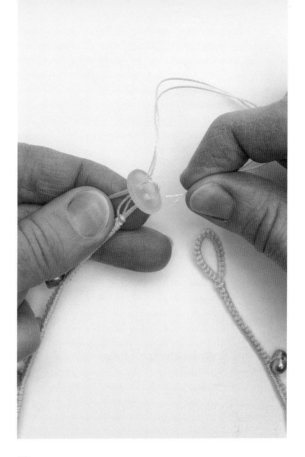

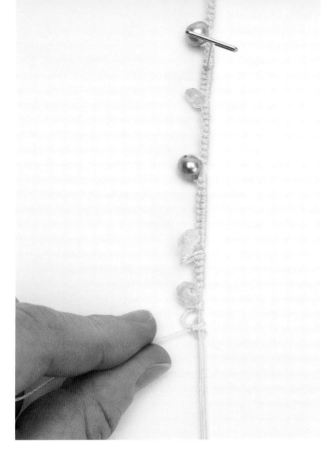

6. To complete the knot, make a second loop for the lark's head knot, pulling this one tight as shown. Continue adding stones followed with a picot after each until you have 7 stones and 7 picots.

7. After adding the seventh stone and picot, repeat the pattern from the other side of the necklace, tying 10 knots between alternating pearls and stones. Finish by tying about 1½" of knots as you did at the beginning. Attach the button for the closure by separating 4 cords into 2 cords each. Bring 2 cords up through one hole and 2 through the other hole. Bring them back down through the opposite holes from each other and pull to tighten. Tie the ends of the cords together on the back side of the button with a square knot. Clip the ends and glue the knot to secure.

8. To form the net pattern, tie strands of cord to the choker. Cut 9 cords, each one 18" long. Fold each cord in half and attach 7 of them to each of the picot "loops" with a lark's head knot. Attach the remaining 2 cords on either side of the 7 stones: Fold each cord in half, then, using a tooth-pick or small crochet hook, thread the middle of the cord through the knots (somewhere between the last pearl and the picot and stone on the end). It may be tight, but the cord will pass through the knots. Bring the ends through with a lark's head knot to attach. Now you have 18 strands of cord hanging from the middle of the necklace.

9. The net pattern is formed by tying the cords with alternating square knots, and decreasing each row of knots to create a design that is longer in the center (forming a V shape or triangle). Pin the middle of the necklace to a board with a T-pin on each side. Pull all of the cords straight down to work with. Pull the very first and very last cord aside; these will not be used to form the knots. Simply add a stone bead to each of these end cords and tie an overhand knot about 1" down in length to secure the bead. (In this photo you can see the stone bead added to the last cord on the right; the left side does not have a bead yet.) Begin by adding a stone bead to every strand (16 beads). Take the second and third cords (with a bead added to each) and tie them together with a square knot under the beads. Continue along the row, tying 2 cords together for each knot for a total of 8 square knots. This photo shows the first row of alternating knots being tied.

10. For the next row, add 14 beads to the middle cords (leave a bead off the first and last cord). Tie alternating square knots *between* each of the previous 8 knots, for a total of 7 knots. This photo shows the middle knot being tied. For the third row, add 10 beads to the 10 middle cords. Tie alternating knots under the 10 beads, leaving the cords on each end loose as the work decreases. For the final row, tie just 2 beads with the middle 2 cords. The knot tied under these two beads will fall in the center of the work.

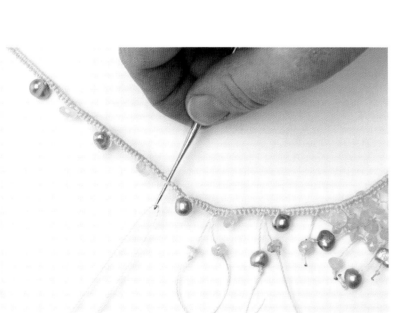

11. Above: Add pearls and stone beads to the end of each cord. Alternate the pearls and stones, tying a barrel knot under each bead to secure. The knots are placed at varying lengths to give the necklace personality. Clip the ends and melt with a wax-heating tool for a neat finish.

12. Left: If you want to add a few extra strands, use the scraps of cord and thread them along the necklace with a small crochet hook to pull the cord through the knots. Tie the cord with a lark's head knot and add beads or pearls to the ends of the cords, finishing them as you did in step 11.

OCEAN BLUE BRACELET

This project uses the same materials as the mermaid necklace and is formed in similar fashion. Cut one piece of cord 1 yard long (core cord) and one piece 4 yards long (working cord). Match the ends of both cords so that they are even and begin tying a sennit of lark's head knots at the midpoint of the 1-yard piece (about 18" from the ends, with the longer cord tying around the shorter core cord). Make a loop as described in steps 1–2 for the mermaid necklace. After forming the loop for the closure you will now have 4 cords at the base of the loop. The longest cord will be the working cord to tie

around the remaining 3 cords (serving as the core). To form the bracelet, tie a sennit of lark's head knots with the single working cord around the bundle of 3 core cords for about ½". Add a stone bead to the working cord and tie 2 lark's heads knots following the bead. The pattern for this bracelet alternates a pearl followed by 3 stone beads. Each stone and pearl is separated by 2 knots. As soon as the bracelet fits around your wrist, finish by adding a few more knots without beads. Add a button as described in step 7 for the necklace.

materials

- 1 roll J. & P. Coats & Clark nylon crochet cord
- 1 Dritz Glamour Ring (2¼" diameter)
- Assorted beads (21–30, depending on how long the belt is) with large holes
- Small piece of wire for threading beads

Beaded Belt

For this pattern it is helpful to always number your cords from left to right (in this case, 1 to 16), renumbering them as they shift. This way you can know which cord to knot to form the pattern. It's also helpful to think of tying knots in terms of rows. Knots that are placed next to each other horizontally are in the same row. A knot tied under or below another knot, even diagonally in position to the previous, is considered a new row.

This belt is made with nylon crochet cord, which is inexpensive and lends itself well to macramé techniques.

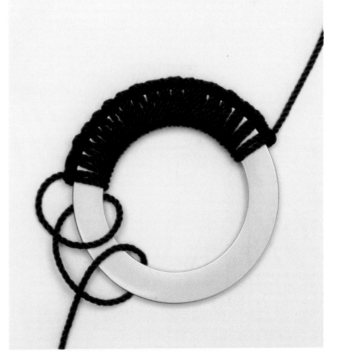

1. Cut one piece of cord 8 yards long, and 7 pieces 6 yards long each. To begin, fold the longest cord (8 yards) in half and attach it to the ring with a lark's head knot. An equal number of knots will be tied from the cords on each side of this knot to cover the ring in both directions.

2. With one of end of the cord, make 19 lark's head knots in one direction. With the other end of the cord, do the same, working in the opposite direction. When finished you will have 39 lark's head knots total.

Lark's head knot	Alternating square knots	Double half hitch	Square knot	Overhand knot

KNOTS

3. Secure the belt loop to a board with a binder clip. Attach the remaining 7 cords, placing them between the 2 end cords used to cover the ring. Fold each in half and tie with a lark's head knot until the ring is completely covered. You now have 16 cords in all to form the macramé pattern for the belt.

4. Begin by making an alternating square knot pattern. Starting with the first 4 cords on the left, tie the first square knot.

5. Repeat with the remaining cords to form a row of 4 square knots, using 4 cords for each.

7. Form the third row, tying 4 square knots across as you did for the first row. Continue this pattern until you have 5 rows of knots total, ending with a row of 4 knots.

8. Pull cords #1 and 2 off to the left side, and tie a square knot using cords #3, 4, 5, and 6.

6. For the next row, pull aside the first 2 cords at far left and at far right. With the other 12 cords, tie 3 square knots, using alternating cords between the knots from the previous row.

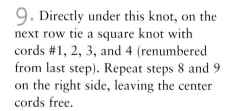

9. Directly under this knot, on the next row tie a square knot with cords #1, 2, 3, and 4 (renumbered from last step). Repeat steps 8 and 9 on the right side, leaving the center cords free.

11. Left: Place pins in your work to hold the knots securely before beginning the double half hitches. (You'll want to add pins to secure your work in successive stages.) Looking at the cords hanging straight down, number them from 1 to 16. Bring cord #9 across the left side at a 45-degree angle and pin into place. This becomes the holding cord. Tie cord #8 over #9 with a double half hitch.

10. This photo shows the knot pattern on both sides.

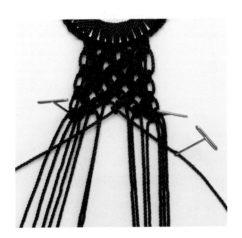

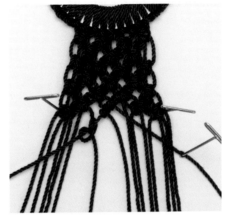

12. Bring cord #8 (the cord you just knotted with) across the 7 cords on the right at a 45-degree angle and pin in place. This will become the holding cord for the knots on the right side of the design.

13. Working leftward from the center, tie double half hitch knots over holding cord #9 with cords #7 through #1.

14. This photo shows the completed left side of double half hitch knots tied to the holding cord.

15. Left: Repeat on the right side, tying cord #10 over the #8 holding cord, and proceed to tie cords #11 through #16 over the same holding cord. Tighten up the knots to neaten, pulling the cords straight down. The finished pattern of double half hitch knots looks like an inverted V.

16. Add a large bead to one of the center cords. Bend a small wire to pull a doubled piece of cord through the bead's hole. Secure the bead on each side with an overhand knot.

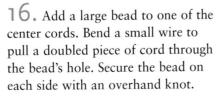

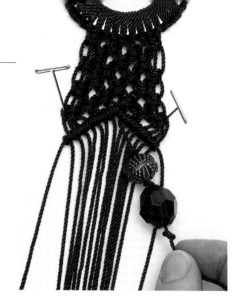

17. Add a bead or two to either side of the center bead previously added and secure on each side with an overhand knot. It doesn't matter which cord you use; simply choose one near the center of the pattern. Make a decision based on the size of the beads or how close you want them near the center bead.

18. Place a pin on each side of your work about 1½–2" down from the double half hitch knots. This will hold the cords to begin the next section of double half hitch knots, which will form a V shape. Divide the cords in half (8 on each side); start on the left and pull cord #1 across at a 45-degree angle and pin.

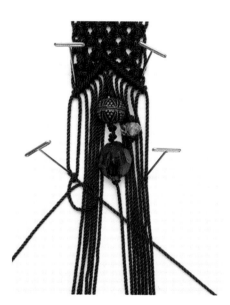

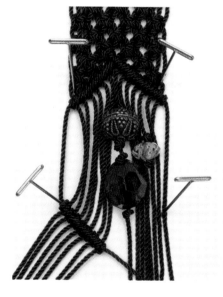

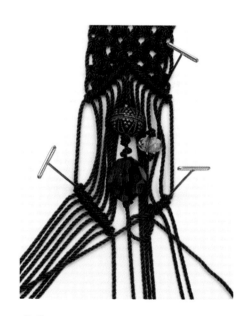

19. Tie double half hitches starting with cord #2, knotting each over the holding cord and ending with #8.

20. Move to the right side. Pull cord #16 across, pin it at a 45-degree angle, and tie double half hitches toward the center with cords #15 through #9.

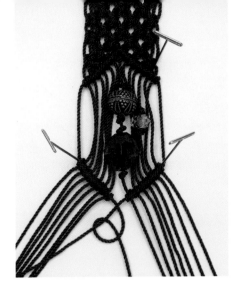

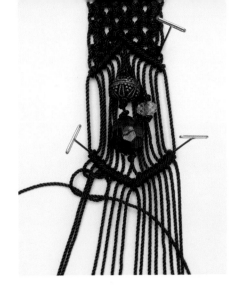

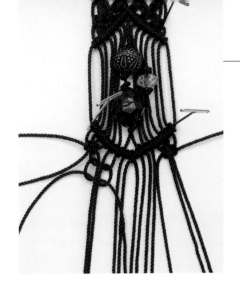

21. To connect the two series of knots that will form the point of the V shape, tie holding cord #1 with a double half hitch around cord #16. Pull the knot tight in the center.

22. Pull all of the cords straight down and start a pattern of alternating square knots, reversing the pattern from the previous steps by increasing the knots for each row, rather than decreasing. Tie a square knot using cords #1 through #4 on the left and cords #12 through #16 on the right.

23. Pull cords #1 and #2 out of the way off to the left and #15 and #16 off to the right of the design and tie a square knot on each side. The left knot uses cords #3, 4, 5, and 6 and the right knot is tied with cords #11, 12, 13, and 14.

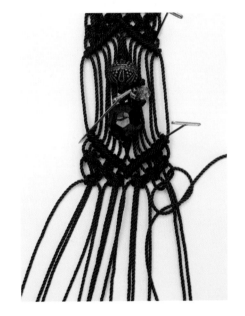

24. For the third row, tie a row of 4 square knots across, followed by a row of 3 knots, and then 4 knots across. After 5 rows the pattern repeats with step 5 to form the open V.

25. You will count 9 rows in all, 2 rows with one knot on each side, 5 rows of alternating knots, then 2 rows with one knot on each side. Repeat steps 11 through 21, reproducing the pattern to form the belt.

26. Measure the belt around your waist. Stop the bead pattern, then tie rows of alternating square knots until the belt fits, plus a few extra inches. Using 2 cords for each, tie 8 overhand knots at the base of the square knots to finish. Leave long strands of the cord for tying to the ring; melt their ends with a wax-heating tool. To wear the belt, loop the ends of the cord through the ring.

materials

- 13 yards brown C-Lon cord (#18-gauge nylon)

- Large turquoise nugget for clasp

- Small faceted silver beads, about 3 mm each (I used 56, but again, the number will depend on wrist size)

- Round turquoise beads, 5–6 mm (I used 28 here, but the specific number depends on wrist size)

- Small-gauge wire, bent in half to act as a beading needle

Turquoise and Silver Bracelet

This bracelet of turquoise and silver combined with a warm brown earth tone is reminiscent of Southwestern style. A large turquoise nugget is used for a closure. As a variation you could use a silver concha-style button for a closure instead.

1. Cut 6 pieces of cord: one 3 yards long and 5 that are 2 yards long each. Set 2 of the 2-yard cords aside to use in step 5. Find the midpoint of the long cord and 3 of the shorter cords and start tying a sennit of lark's head knots about 6" above the midpoint, using the longest cord to tie knots over the other 3 (core) cords. Form this chain of knots into a loop to serve as the closure of the bracelet. When the turquoise nugget fits through the loop, stop tying knots.

2. With the top of the loop clipped to a board, tie a square knot under the loop, using 2 cords from each side to tie the knot over the 4 cords in the middle.

Lark's head knot/ sennit	Square knot	Double half hitch

KNOTS

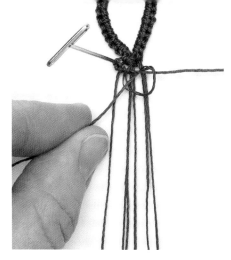

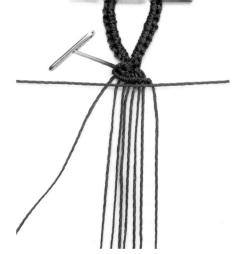

3. Bring the first cord on the left horizontally across the rest of the cords. Use a pin to hold it at left as shown. Use a piece of tape or a clip to secure the end of the cord on the right-hand side. This cord will act as the holding cord around which double half hitch knots will be tied.

4. Begin tying double half hitch knots over the holding cord starting with cord #2 and working to the last cord on the right (#8).

5. To increase the number of cords in the pattern, introduce a new cord (one of the reserved 2-yard cords). Pin it horizontally under the row of double half hitches.

6. Tie each of the cords over the new cord with double half hitches, working left to right.

7. Add the second reserved cord to increase again, tying half hitches over it as you did in step 6.

8. You now have 12 cords to macramé with.

9. Left: Add a small silver bead to the second cord on the left side. Use one cord on each side of this cord to tie a square knot under the bead. This photo shows the first half-knot of the square knot.

10. Right: Add 3 more silver beads for a total of 4 in a row with the rest of the cords as shown.

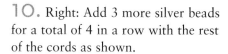

11. Add a turquoise bead to each of the same core cords to which you added the silver beads. Tie a firm square knot under each bead.

12. Add another silver bead to each of the same core cords under each turquoise bead; however, do not tie a knot underneath. Bring the first cord (#1) on the left across horizontally; make sure it is under the silver beads. Hold it in position at left with a pin. Tape or clip the tail of the cord on the right side. This becomes the holding cord for a row of double half hitches.

13. Tie double half hitch knots starting with cord #2, knotting each cord over the holding cord until the last one on the right is tied.

14. To make a second row of double half hitches, bring the holding cord (same one used in the preceding step) across the cords to the left. Pin the right-hand side to hold the cord in place and clip or tape its end to the left.

15. For this row of double half hitch knots, tie each cord over the holding cord in the same manner as for the previous row, except now working right to left, the opposite direction from step 13.

16. This photo shows the pattern for the bracelet so far. At this point, repeat steps 9 through 15 to continue the pattern until the bracelet fits around your wrist. You will be adding a few extra rows for the closure, so keep that in mind as you check the fit.

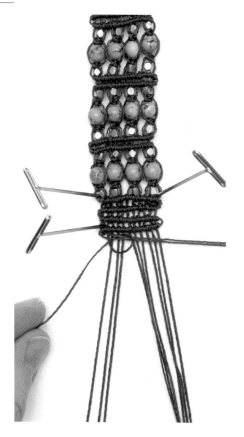

17. Left: To make a handsome finish for the closure, add two more rows of half hitches. At the beginning of the design, cords were added to increase the number of working cords. Now you will decrease the number for a nice tapered look to match the opposite end. To decrease: Split the cords, dividing them down the middle. Pull the last 6 cords over to the right and set aside. Bring the first 2 cords from the left side across the 4 cords next to them. These 2 cords will act together as though they were one holding cord. Tie double half hitches over both cords (#1 and #2) with each of the 4 cords on the left side, working left to right.

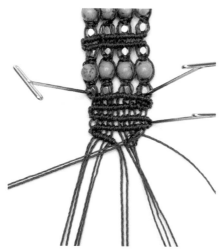

18. Above: Repeat the same process as in step 17, this time on the opposite side, working right to left. Remember to use the last 2 cords as though they were one holding cord.

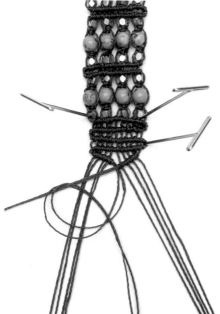

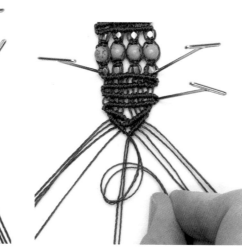

19. Tie the 2 holding cords from the left side over the 2 holding cords from the right with a double half hitch to secure them in the center.

20. Repeat steps 17 through 19 to make one more set of double half hitch rows.

21. Make sure the center is pulled tightly for the last knot.

22. Use the 4 cords in the center to attach the large nugget bead. Thread 2 cord ends through the left side and 2 cords through the right, then pull the ends.

23. Use a small piece of wire or large needle to thread the same ends of the cord coming from the bead back through the knots to the back side of the bracelet.

24. Flip the bracelet over and tie the cords with a square knot.

25. Clip off the ends of the knot and the ends of the rest of the cords. Melt the ends with a wax-heating tool to prevent fraying and to secure the knots.

materials

- 12 yards pink C-Lon cord
- Watch face with bars to attach band
- 2 silver beads, 6–8 mm each
- 60 or more "E" beads (6/0-size seed beads)
- 6 or more charms
- Alphabet beads
- Button for closure
- Large needle for finishing ends of cord

WATCHBAND

Express yourself with a funky watchband in your favorite color. Add charms or beads to embellish the design. Watch faces are available online or through bead and jewelry suppliers. Before purchasing a watch face, make sure you can attach cord to the finding.

1. Cut the cord into 12 equal-size pieces. Fold 6 cords in half and attach each to one watchband bar with a lark's head knot. You now have 12 strands to work with. Following steps 3 and 4 of the preceding turquoise-and-silver bracelet project, tie a row of double half hitch knots from left to right, then tie a second row of double half hitches, this time from right to left. When you're done with this row, slide a silver bead over the 2 center cords, then divide the cords into 2 equal groups. Bring the leftmost cord diagonally across the left group of cords to act as a holding cord, and tie the rest on the left with double half hitches until you reach the middle, to finish this side. Repeat the process on the right side. When you reach the middle, tie the cords in the center to connect. Continue in this manner, adding another row of knots on each side, then connect the last knot in the middle.

Lark's head knot   Double half hitch   Square knot

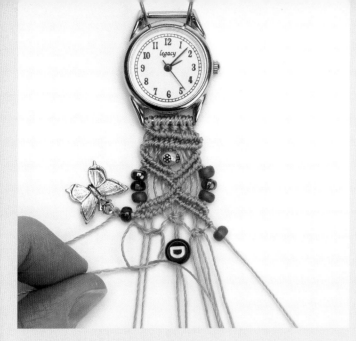

2. Add 3 "E" beads to each leftmost and rightmost cord. Starting from the center, bring cord #6 diagonally to the left to act as a holding cord for a series of double half hitches beginning with cord #5. Continue tying knots from the center, working right to left until the cord with the beads on the left side is tied on last. Repeat the pattern on the right side, working from the opposite direction. Then create a second row of knots on each side in the same manner. Next, add a bead to the first cord at left, followed by a charm. Add a bead to the last cord on the far right. Pull these cords aside. Tie a square knot with the 4 cords in the center, using 2 for holding cords and the other 2 to tie the knot. Slide a letter bead over the 2 center cords. Tie a square knot on each side of the letter using 4 cords for each knot. Notice that the knotting cords from the first square knot are used to form each of these side knots. Tie another square knot under the letter bead.

3. Add another bead to the leftmost cord following the charm. Bring the cord diagonally back across to the middle and tie a row of double half hitch knots. Add another bead to the rightmost cord and repeat the pattern on the right side, working in the opposite direction. Repeat the overall knot-bead-charm pattern until the watchband fits around half your wrist. Create the other half of the watchband in the same manner with the remaining 6 cords.

4. Far left: To finish the ends, on one side of the band, divide the cords into 2 groups of 6 and tie a sennit of square knots on each side, using 2 cords as the core and 2 for tying, until together the two sennits form a loop big enough for the button. Tie all the cords together with a square knot to make the loop. With a large needle, weave the ends of the cord back through the work to hide them. Clip off the ends and glue the knot to secure. Melt the cut ends of cord with a wax-heating tool.

5. Near left: Add a button to the other end of the watchband by bringing a couple of cords through the shank of the button (2 cords each running opposite through the shank). Thread them through to the back side of the work and tie with a square knot. Clip off the ends and glue or melt to secure. The extra cords left can be cut near the double half hitches and melted as well.

materials

- 1 skein Lion Brand Wool-Ease Chunky yarn, color Grass 130
- 1 ball Lion Brand Incredible ribbon yarn, color Purple Party 207
- Wood purse handles with beads (Bag Boutique #9803 by Prym)
- Corrugated cardboard, cut to the width of the purse
- Small piece of wire for threading beads
- Large plastic craft beads, multiple colors

Variegated Ribbon Yarn Purse

A purse or a handbag is a perfect project to take advantage of the fact that you can macramé with almost any fiber. An alternating square knot makes a woven texture for the purse; it can be knotted to create a solid pattern or spaced apart for a "netted," loose-weave effect.

The purse handles come with a beaded portion, which you can use as is if you prefer. However, for this project, I've replaced them with beaded ribbons to match the purse.

1. Cut 36 lengths of Chunky yarn and 36 lengths of ribbon yarn, each 2½ yards long. Pair one piece of yarn with one piece of ribbon; you will work these together as though they were one cord. Find the midpoint of a yarn-ribbon pair and fold it in half, then attach to one handle with a lark's head knot. Continue with 17 more pairs. Repeat the knots on the other handle. Each handle will have 18 knots across.

2. Attach the top of one handle to a board with a binder clip. From this point on, the yarn-ribbon pair will be referred to as *one* cord. The macramé pattern for the purse consists of alternating square knots. Take the first 4 cords on the left side and tie a square knot (this will use the first two lark's head knots on the handle). Proceed to tie square knots along the row, completing 9 knots across.

| Lark's head knot | Alternating square knots | Overhand knot |

KNOTS

3. For the next row, pull the first 2 cords on the left out to the side and tie alternating square knots with the remaining cords. There will be 8 knots along the row, one knot between each of the knots in the previous row.

4. After completing 3 rows (the third one ends with a row of 9 knots), finish 3 rows on the other handle. To attach the two sections to form the purse, cut a piece of corrugated cardboard the width of the purse handles and a little longer than you want the length of the purse to be (about 14" long). Place the handles on opposite sides of the cardboard, matching the tops and sides. With binder clips, secure both sides of the woven knots to the cardboard. This will keep the sides even and prevent shifting as you work. To form the body of the purse, you will be tying knots all the way around the cardboard. Begin by taking the 2 cords from the end of the row on one side, and 2 from the other. Tie a square knot to join the two sections on the side of the cardboard as shown.

5. Continue tying alternating square knots all the way around the cardboard until you are happy with the length of the purse. Leave at least 6" of cord remaining at the bottom. This photo shows the pattern of knots, with an alternating square knot being tied with 2 cords from one knot and 2 from the previous row.

6. To form the bottom, unclip the purse, remove the cardboard, and turn inside out. Take one strand from one side of the purse and tie it with a square knot to the knot directly across from it. Continue tying knots to close the bottom of the purse. Clip the ends of the cord about 1" from the knots. Seal each end with hem sealant or fabric glue.

7. To make the strap, cut 4 ribbons, each about 1½ yards long. Take one ribbon and fold in half. Attach through the hole on the purse handle with a lark's head knot.

8. Thread large beads over both ends of the ribbon, using a wire to aid threading.

9. Tie an overhand knot on both sides of each bead threaded.

10. Use another strand of ribbon to attach a large bead to the front of the purse, looping it through the macramé knots near the top center. Knot a few extra ribbons at the base of the bead for decoration using an overhand knot.

materials

▶ 1 skein Darice wool-blend hemp yarn, 2-ply worsted weight

▶ Piece of corrugated cardboard, 2¾ x 5"

▶ 3 wood beads, any size

▶ Piece of felt, 6 x 5"

▶ Sewing needle and thread

▶ 1 wood button, any size

▶ Fabric sealant

iPod Pouch

Make a small pouch to fit any small accessory or electronic device by simply measuring the item to create your own pattern. Add fabric or felt to line the inside of the macramé pouch for a professional and sturdy finish. This is definitely one project that is far removed from the old jute plant hangers that were so popular in the 1970s.

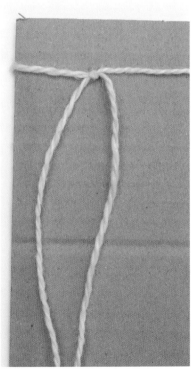

1. Far left: Cut one strand of yarn 20" long to serve as the holding cord. Cut 29 strands of yarn 60" long each. Set one of the strands aside to use for the strap, described in step 15. To begin, wrap the 20" holding cord around the top of the iPod, tying it in the center with a square knot. The knotting cords will be tied to this to form the pouch. The ends of the yarn that extend from the knot should be equal in length.

2. Near left: Cut a piece of cardboard the same width as and a little longer than the iPod (this one is 2¾ x 5"). Transfer the holding cord to the top of the cardboard. Pull the knot to one side and the ends of the yarn up out of the way as you work (these will be used later to form the strap).

Square knot	Lark's head knot/ sennit	Alternating square knots/sennit	Double half hitch	Overhand knot	
					KNOTS

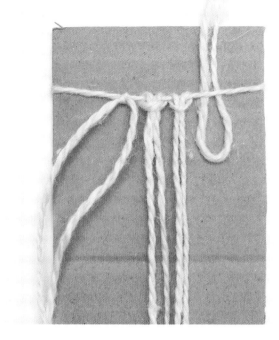

3. Attach the remaining 28 strands to the holding cord (14 strands on each side of the cardboard), tying each with a lark's head knot at the center of each cord to secure.

4. Secure the holding cord to the top of the cardboard with a binder clip. Starting from the left on one side of the cardboard, tie the first 4 cords with a square knot. Continue down the row until you have 7 square knots. Tie the same number of knots on the other side of the cardboard. Take the middle two cords (from knot #4 in the row of attached knots) and slide a wood bead over them. Repeat on the other side of the cardboard.

5. For the second row, begin tying alternating square knots. On this row, you will begin to decrease the number of knots to allow for the diagonal pattern of double half hitches. Starting on the left, tie 2 square knots, with one knot between the first and second knots and one between the second and third knots of the previous (first) row. Tie the same number on the right side, leaving the middle section untied. Flip the cardboard over and repeat the same pattern on the back. You will notice that you have 2 cords loose at the far left and far right of each row. Form a square knot on the left-hand edge of the cardboard by bringing 2 cords from the front side and 2 from the back. Do the same on the right-hand edge. This will connect the front and back rows, with alternating knots tied all the way around the cardboard. This completes the second row.

6. For the third row, tie 2 square knots on each side, in the same position as knots #1 and #2 from the first row, leaving the middle section open. After the third row, to form a diamond shape around the bead, first bring the left strand from the central square knot across to the left, holding it diagonally under the 3 decreasing square knots. This will become the holding cord.

7. Tie 6 double half hitch knots, working right to left.

8. Repeat the double half hitch knots on the right side to form a mirror image of the left side.

9. Bring the holding cord from the left side diagonally to the right and back down to the center. Tie 7 double half hitches (this includes one of the strands from the center bead).

10. Repeat the pattern on the right side to complete the diamond. As you come to the center, join the base of the diamond by tying one last knot to connect.

11. Repeat the diamond pattern on the back side of the pouch. Tie alternating square knots to fill in the area around the diamond, this time increasing the number, with the seventh row of alternating knots matching the first row.

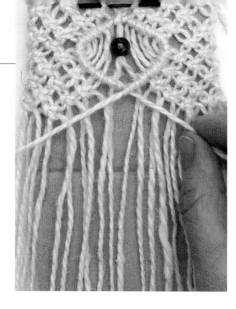

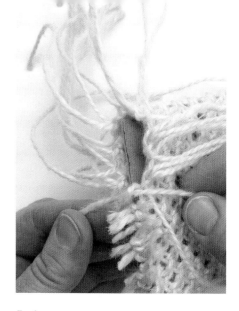

12. Repeat the double half hitch diamond pattern as described in steps 7 through 10, with a wood bead in the center of the diamond. This photo shows the holding cords before the knots are tied.

13. Continue the pattern until you have 3 diamond shapes, each of these sections incorporating a wood bead. Finish the length of the pouch with rows of alternating square knots. This pouch has 23 rows total from top to bottom, but measure the iPod as you work to make sure the length is correct.

14. After completing the rows, remove the cardboard and turn the work inside out. Form the bottom of the pouch by tying opposite strands from each side with square knots. Clip the cord ends about ½" from the knots and secure with fabric sealant.

15. To make a strap to fit over the top width of the pouch, fold the reserved 60" strand of yarn in half and, with a lark's head knot, tie it to the holding cord at the top of the pouch, directly over the tails of the square knot you made in the holding cord at the beginning of the project. You now have two 30"-long pieces of yarn, plus 2 tail cords from the knot tied at the beginning, with which to work.

16. Using these 30" lengths of yarn, tie a sennit of a few square knots over the tail ends (which will act as core cords), and then set aside to finish after the lining is added.

17. To prevent the yarn or beads from scratching the iPod screen and to give the pouch stability and structure, make a lining using a piece of felt cut to 6 x 5". Fold this in half to make it 3 x 5". Using regular sewing thread, stitch up, by hand or machine, the 5" side and across the 3" width for the bottom with a ¼" seam allowance; trim close to the seam and clip the corner diagonally where the seams meet. To give the lining dimension, form the corners into a point and stitch across the corner, measuring ¼" from each point to accommodate the thickness of the iPod. Clip off the points. Measure the lining with the knotted pouch and trim the top of the lining so that it is a little bit shorter in length than the pouch. Check the fit for the iPod.

18. With the pouch still turned inside out, slip the pouch inside the lining so that the "wrong" sides (sides with the seams and rough edges) are facing together.

19. With a needle and thread, whipstitch the top of the felt lining to the macraméd pouch.

20. Turn the pouch right side out. Near the top, sew, through the felt layer and macramé knots, a wood button to the side opposite the strap. Place the iPod in the pouch and bring the strap over the top to check its length. Tie extra square knots to complete the strap until you reach the button. To finish, split the 2 strands into 2 on each side. Tie a lark's head sennit on each side to make a buttonhole.

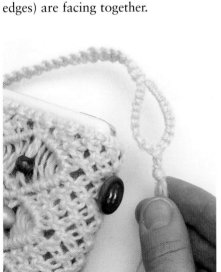

21. Measure to fit over the button. Tie a square knot followed by an overhand knot with all four strands to complete. Clip off the end and secure the knot with fabric sealant.

Resources

You can find most of the supplies used in beading and macramé at your local craft or bead retailer, which can assist you with product selection, offer advice when you need help, or order something for you if they don't have it in stock.

The suppliers listed below are offered as additional resources, in the event you can't find a store in your area that carries a particular item or will accept a request for an order.

Enchanting Beads

P.O. Box 905
Lillian, AL 36549
www.enchantingbeads.com
Large-holed beads, leather cord

Jane's Fiber & Beads

5415 East Andrew Johnson Highway
P.O. Box 110
Afton, TN 37616
1-888-497-2665 (toll-free)
1-423-639-7919
www.janesfiberandbeads.com
Chinese knotting cord, C-Lon cord

Kirsten Peters McGrath

6043 N. Forkner
Fresno, CA 93711
www.fcocdesign.com
Lampwork beads

Moondance Designs

1377 Old Marlboro Road
Concord, MA 01742-4738
E-mail: tguthrie@moondancedesigns.com
www.moondancedesigns.com
C-Lon and Mastex cord

Sherri Haab Designs

1-801-489-3885
www.sherrihaab.com
Handmade charms and bezels, jewelry kits

Index

Other Jewelrymaking Books by Sherri Haab

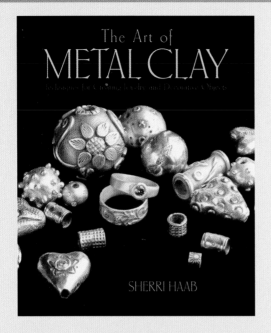

The Art of Metal Clay

A comprehensive introduction to the medium—detailing the essentials of working, firing, and finishing—that also demonstrates how it can be textured, molded, carved, and sculpted to create beads, bracelets, pendants, earrings, rings and other jewelry settings, boxes and vessels, and mixed-media pieces that incorporate glass, epoxy resin, and polymer clay.

ISBN 0-8230-0367-1
ISBN-13: 978-0-8230-0367-9

The Art of Resin Jewelry

Shows how to use resin to create beautiful necklaces, bangles, bracelets, pins, earrings, and rings. Instructions include how to add colorants and other materials, how to cast three-dimensional forms, and how to combine resin with polymer clay.

ISBN 0-8230-0344-2
ISBN-13: 978-0-8230-0344-0

Designer Style Jewelry

Features the latest techniques for making stunning jewelry out of wire, beads, polymer clay, leather, resin, laminate, shrink plastic, and more, along with illustrated, step-by-step projects for earrings, necklaces, pendants, pins, bracelets, and rings.

ISBN 0-8230-2601-9
ISBN-13: 978-0-8230-2601-2

WATSON-GUPTILL PUBLICATIONS
www.watsonguptill.com